Insight Group

MW01453761

Workbook
Updated Edition

By Jimmy Ray Lee, D.Min.

Communications should be addressed to:
Turning Point Ministries, Inc.
P. O. Box 22127
Chattanooga, TN 37422-2127

ISBN 10: 1-58119-092-1
ISBN 13: 978-1-58119-092-2

Produced by

Turning Point®

About the Author

Dr. Jimmy Ray Lee is the founder and president of Turning Point Ministries, Inc. He is the author of *Understanding the Times* and several small group studies published by Turning Point Ministries. Under the direction and guidance of Dr. Lee, Turning Point produced Living Free—a high impact, video-based training. This training helps churches develop Christ-centered small groups that deal with the contemporary problems that people face today.

Dr. Lee is the founder and honorary chairman of Project 714 (now known as National Center for Youth Issues), a chemical prevention/intervention program for schools. He also founded an inner-city ministry called Ark Ministries that reached 600 to 700 young people weekly. He started the Chattanooga Teen Challenge and served as its president for three years. Jimmy served as Nashville Teen Challenge executive director during its formative years.

In 1983 he was awarded the "Service to Mankind Award" presented by the Highland Sertoma Club in Hixson, Tennessee.

Insight Group

Contents

Workbook: *Insight Group*, Turning Point, P. O. Box 22127, Chattanooga, TN 37422-2127

Introduction

To the Insight Group

Welcome to the *Insight Group*. The *Insight Group* is for people who need help to stay free from life-controlling problems. A life-controlling problem is anything that masters a person's life. The apostle Paul writes, "I will not be mastered by anything" (1 Corinthians 6:12).

The purpose of the *Insight Group* is to help each participant "walk in the way of understanding" (Proverbs 9:6) as it relates to an individual who is struggling with a life-controlling problem or one who wants to learn how to avoid such a mastering problem. The main goal of the *Insight Group* is to assist group members along the path of total recovery—physically, emotionally, and spiritually—from their problems and to encourage them to grow in the grace and knowledge of Jesus Christ.

Since most people—if not all—are dealing with some area of struggle, the *Insight Group* can benefit any person who is open to the Lord's working in their life. It can help group members discover how life-controlling problems develop and learn how to identify the spiritual and emotional conditions that contribute to a problem's taking root and growing in one's life or in the life of someone they know.

The group should meet each week for one hour and fifteen minutes, but more time may be planned if necessary. The material is designed for nine sessions.

It is important to note that the *Insight Group* is not a substitute for medical or psychological care. Participants should not be advised to stop taking medication or discontinue their doctor's care.

At the conclusion of the course, check into opportunities to join another Living Free group.

It is our prayer that through participation in and completing this study, you will have a greater understanding of the freedom you have in Christ.

Please be faithful in your attendance at each group meeting and do the assignments in your group member guide before each group session. This workbook will help prepare you for each session.

As you and the small group walk together through this study, may you discover complete freedom to grow in Christ.

The Insight Group can benefit any person who is open to the Lord's working in their life.

Session 1 Orientation

Personal Preparation: Getting Ready for Session One

Welcome

Personal Notes

Welcome to our *Insight Group*. You have taken a positive step. We thank God for your participation.

During this course, there will be suggested time alone with God in meditation, prayer, and scripture reading. This time with God is vital to our spiritual growth. We encourage you to be faithful in your devotion time with the Lord.

For this session, read 2 Peter 1.

Sharing Question
Welcome to our first *Insight Group* meeting. I would like to begin this first session by having each of us in the group introduce ourselves. I will start by telling you that my name is....

Self-Awareness

We are glad for each of you who has joined this group. And in case you are not entirely sure of what you have joined, I am going to take a minute to tell you what an *Insight Group* is.

The front cover of this guide is subtitled: *Discover the Path to Christian Character*. We sometimes face roadblocks in our quest to become less isolated and move toward better relationships with each other and with God. These roadblocks or walls are what we refer to as life-controlling issues or problems.

There is hope! Discovering an insight into how these problems develop is the first step leading to how they can be overcome by building on qualities that strengthen us on the "path to Christian character."

An *Insight Group* is a small group (usually 12 people or fewer) who wants to either get free or stay free from life-controlling problems or who want to discover more about the potential we all have for developing such a problem.

Workbook: *Insight Group*, Turning Point, P. O. Box 22127, Chattanooga, TN 37422-2127

We define a life-controlling problem as anything that masters (or controls) a person's life. Many terms have been used to describe life-controlling problems. Someone may speak of a "dependency," a "compulsive behavior," or an "addiction." In 2 Corinthians 10:4, the Apostle Paul uses the word *stronghold* to describe an area of sin that has become a part of our lifestyle when he writes that there is "divine power to demolish strongholds."

The easiest life-controlling problems to identify are harmful habits like drug or alcohol use, eating disorders, sexual addictions, gambling, tobacco use, and the like. But life-controlling problems can also include harmful feelings like anger and fear.

The word *addiction* or *dependency* can refer to the use of a substance (like food, alcohol, legal and/or illegal drugs, and others), or it can refer to the practice of a behavior (like shoplifting, gambling, pornography use, compulsive spending, TV watching, and others), or it can involve a relationship with another person which we call "co-dependencies."

The Apostle Paul talks about life-controlling problems in terms of our being "slaves" to this behavior or dependency that masters us. He writes in Romans 6:14, "Sin shall not be your master." In 1 Corinthians 6:12 he says, "Everything is permissible for me—but I will not be mastered by anything [or anyone]."

Second Peter 2:19 says, "For a man is a slave to whatever has mastered him." Anything that becomes the center of a life—if allowed to continue—will become master of that life.

Why is the *Insight Group* for everyone? Because we live in a world today that can be described as an addictive society. Most people are affected in some way by a life-controlling problem—their own or someone else's.

It is important to note that life-controlling problems do not happen overnight. There are predictable steps with certain characteristics associated with each one. During the next few weeks, our goal is to help you detect those steps and stop the progress of a mastering substance or behavior. Please understand that we look to the Lord for help. We want to be channels of God's love.

All people have the potential of being mastered by a life-controlling problem. No one plans for it to happen, but without warning, individuals (and the people who care about them) can be pulled into the downward spiral of a stronghold. Since most people are struggling in some area, this group can benefit any person who is open to the Lord's working in their life.

Group Format

So what will we do here each week as we begin to deal with those life-controlling problems and their consequences? Let me start by giving you an idea of what will happen during a typical meeting.

Introduction

First, we will pray together. Prayer is always appropriate during an *Insight Group* meeting, especially as we begin our time together. We will spend a few minutes talking together and getting to know each other better. We do not want to be a circle of strangers. But in saying that, I want to be quick to promise you that in any of our conversations here, you should never feel pressured to talk. We only want you to speak when you feel comfortable in doing so.

Self-Awareness

Next in our meeting comes something we call our "Self-Awareness" time. This part of our meeting is designed to help us discover more about ourselves. During Self-Awareness (about 20 minutes), we will discuss some of the practical issues involved in understanding and dealing with life-controlling problems.

We will look at how they develop and how we can identify the spiritual and emotional issues that contribute to a problem's taking root and growing in our lives and in the lives of the people around us.

Spiritual Awareness

After our Self-Awareness time, we are going to open our Bibles and spend some time working together on the qualities God wants to build into our lives. If you can picture a life-controlling problem as a downward spiral that keeps pulling us deeper and deeper, then the qualities that we will study from God's Word are like a ladder that helps us to climb out of the deep hole of a life-controlling problem.

Maybe this would be a good time to say that our ultimate purpose here is not simply to empty our lives of a particular life-controlling problem we might be struggling with right now. We cannot leave the center of our lives open and undefended because something—maybe an even worse problem—is going to fill it.

So yes, we do want to get rid of dependencies and addictions; but in the process, we want to make *Christ* the center of our lives.

David recognized the need to have God as his tower of strength. He said:

> *The LORD is my rock, my fortress and my deliverer; my God is my rock, in whom I take refuge, my shield and the horn of my salvation. He is my stronghold, my refuge and my Savior* (2 Samuel 22:2-3).

Workbook: *Insight Group*, Turning Point, P. O. Box 22127, Chattanooga, TN 37422-2127

This would be a good time to say that if you have not yet invited Christ into your life, I would encourage you today to ask Him to come into your life as Savior and Lord. You will find more information in the back of this workbook on page 74.

That faith in Christ is going to be the focus of our bible study time next week because it is the foundation of all God wants to do in our lives.

Application
After our bible study, we will take some time to work on applying what we have learned. We want these things we are learning to make a difference in our lives. Our Spiritual Awareness studies as well as the Application time that follows are designed to show us the path for Christian character as it is found in God's Word.

That should give you a general idea of what to expect when you come here each week.

Ground Rules

Here are the basic ground rules for our *Insight Group*.

1. **We want you to be here.** Make every effort to be here. Make these nine sessions a top priority in your life. Each session is important to you, and you are important to this group. In addition to what God wants to do in your life, you have a great deal to contribute to the lives of others in this group. If you cannot attend for some reason, please give one of us a call to let us know.

2. **You should speak within your own comfort level.** I have already mentioned this, but I want to stress that this should be a nonthreatening place. Yes, I am going to throw out a lot of questions. Think about them. Some of you will be ready to talk and answer, but for others it may take a while before you are comfortable. Do not feel pressured.

3. **There is to be confidentiality concerning anything that is shared within the group.** We must be able to trust each other to maintain confidentiality. (I might add here that it is important for us to maintain the confidences of the other people in our lives also. This is not the place to tell what you know about your spouse's problems or your children's or your friend's. (It is not appropriate to gossip.) The only exception to maintaining confidentiality should be when a person is a danger to themselves or others.

4. **Make a commitment to prepare for each session.** You have been given (or will receive) this group member's workbook. It contains some written questions and bible reading assignments that will get you ready for what we'll be doing during our sessions here. Your workbook is a private place—just between you and God. No one else ever needs to read what you have written there. Do take time to let God work in your life during the week as you prepare for our time together.

5. **Spend time alone with God every day.** Included in the workbook are some suggestions for how you might spend approximately thirty minutes a day in Bible reading, meditating on God's Word, and in prayer. That time alone with God could be the most significant element of the healing and the building God wants to do in your life.

6. **Make a commitment to stay free of any dependency that may be or has the potential of mastering your life.** Such substance use or behavioral practice is likely to limit the help you can receive from the group.

7. **Keep in mind that this group is not a substitute for medical or psychological care.** We never advise anyone to stop taking prescribed medications or cancel their doctor's care.

Before we move on to our Spiritual Awareness time, I would like for us to take a few minutes to talk about why we each have come to this *Insight Group*. Maybe you are not totally sure yourself, or you may not yet feel comfortable speaking. That is perfectly okay.

But I am interested to know what circumstances led to your being a part of this group. How did you hear about it? What made you think you wanted to be a part of it?

Spiritual-Awareness

Through the course of our Spiritual Awareness studies, we are going to look at a lot of different Bible verses; but there is one passage we will focus on and return to again and again.

It is a very special portion of God's Word that gets right to the heart of our struggles with the problems that master us. Let's look together at 2 Peter 1:3-11; and before we start to talk about it, let's read it together.

Over the next eight weeks, we will look at eight objectives we find in verses 5 through 7. What are they?

As we study these eight objectives or qualities that God wants to build into our lives, we will see how they build on each other.

For our study this first session, I want us to look at verse 3 and just try to get an overview of the truth that is found in this passage.

THE UPWARD PATH TO DEVELOPING CHRISTIAN CHARACTER

LOVE
KINDNESS
GODLINESS
PERSEVERANCE
SELF-CONTROL
KNOWLEDGE
GOODNESS
FAITH

Workbook: *Insight Group*, Turning Point, P. O. Box 22127, Chattanooga, TN 37422-2127

all things that pertain to life and godliness

What does verse 3 say God has given to us?

His divine power

What is the source of "everything we need"?

We may not have started yet to draw on that power—we certainly have not used it to the fullest extent possible; but for right now, I just want us to see that, here in verse 3, God's Word is telling us that He "has given us *everything we need* for life and godliness."

Move down to verse 4. What does God want to help us escape? corruption that is in the world because of sinful desires

Corruption is decay or rot. It is depravity, perversion, degradation, and contamination. God wants to help us escape all that.

What causes this corruption in the world and in our lives? sinful desires

Evil desires are the urges from our sinful nature that push us toward actions that are harmful to us.

How does verse 4 tell us we can *escape* worldly corruption? He granted us precious and very great promises so that we may become partakers of the divine nature

Meaning what?

Life-controlling problems are a big part of the corruption of our world. Every night on the news, we see stories about people's lives that are being affected by life-controlling problems—their own or someone else's. To a greater or lesser degree, life-controlling problems touch all our lives.

So what is the solution? How can I live free of life-controlling problems? The eight objectives found in 2 Peter 1 hold an important key. As God builds these qualities into our lives, we participate in the divine nature—we become *more* like God and *less* likely to be mastered by a life-controlling problem.

Note how the eight objectives are couched in promises in this chapter:

- "His divine power has given us everything we need" (v.3).
- "Through these he has given us his very great and precious promises" (v.4).
- "They will keep you from being ineffective and unproductive" (v.8).
- "For if you do these things, you will never fall" (v.10).
- "You will receive a rich welcome" (v.11).

Workbook: *Insight Group*, Turning Point, P. O. Box 22127, Chattanooga, TN 37422-2127

It is our prayer that over the weeks ahead you will come to know and love the truth of these verses.

Application

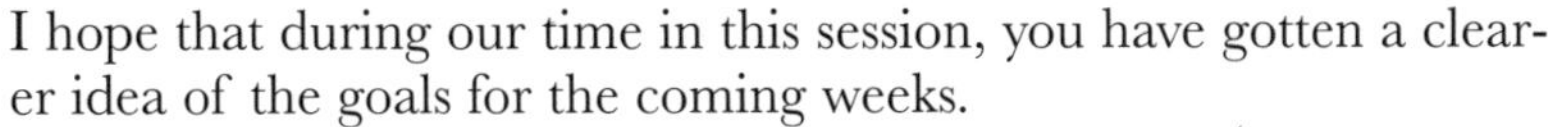

I hope that during our time in this session, you have gotten a clearer idea of the goals for the coming weeks.

As we wrap up our time together, I wonder if you have formulated in your mind an idea of what you want to see happen in your life over the next eight weeks.

What do you want to receive during this course?

Understand how life-controlling problems develop, + grow as well as their effects on lives.
Determine the life-controlling problems that are in my life or could be there.
Root out those present and prevent others from developing.

Workbook: *Insight Group*, Turning Point, P. O. Box 22127, Chattanooga, TN 37422-2127

Session 2 Trust

Personal Preparation: Getting Ready for Session Two

Meet With God

Personal Notes

Our meetings together as a group are important, but God also wants to meet with you alone. Find a quiet place and take some time each day to read from God's word. Think about what you have read and talk to God in prayer.

For this quiet time you will find it helpful to read from Romans 10 and 1 Corinthians 3.

In Session 2 we were introduced to the eight objectives in 2 Peter 1:1-11. In this session we start the journey with our foundation—faith in Christ.

Sharing Question

Who was the most influential person in your childhood and why?
Mom she taught me much - value of honesty
Also Aunts Pauline + Irma who ~~tried~~ to expose me
to the Word

Self-Awareness

Every day of our lives we put our trust in something. I trust that a chair will hold me up. I trust that by turning a key, I can make my car start—usually! I trust the dictionary to give me accurate definitions, and I trust the totals my calculator shows on its display. I trust the bank with my paycheck.

But somehow it is harder to trust people. Probably because, at one time or another, someone has let us down. But to live healthy and productive lives, we need to overcome our reluctance to trust anyone. We need to find people we can trust.

When someone says to you, "Trust me," what thoughts go through your mind? I want to, but must be careful. ~~On~~ spiritual matters, I must ask for the Holy Spirit's help and compare with the Word of God

Workbook: *Insight Group*, Turning Point, P. O. Box 22127, Chattanooga, TN 37422-2127

To help us get to know each other, we are going to take a few minutes to tell a little about ourselves. You can talk about your family, what kind of work you do, what school you went to, what your hobbies are, what your health is like, what you do for fun—whatever you think will help us get to know you better. Describe.

As we spend time together over the weeks ahead and work on some important issues, it's our desire that we will come to trust each other. We hope you will come to feel that this is a "safe place" to express yourself—because we can all trust each other.

Even more important than finding people we can trust is learning to trust God. What are some ways that trust in God and trust in people are *alike?* You can tell them what is on your mind/heart. You believe they give advice they believe is best for you. You can enjoy their company

How are trust in God and trust in people *different?* God is totally trustworthy, He knows all, is all powerful, and all loving

Spiritual Awareness: Faith

Faith

Another way to say "trust in God" is to use the word *faith*. You will remember that during our first session, we briefly identified eight objectives that will result in God's power taking effect in our daily lives. We find them in 2 Peter, chapter 1, verses 3 through 11. Let's turn in our Bibles to 2 Peter...but before we look at those verses, go to the very beginning of this book—or letter—by Peter and see who he is writing to.

Who is Peter addressing? To those who have obtained a faith of equal-standing with ours. Gentiles?

Then we read the promises made to those who have received the faith—found in verses 3 and 4. We talked about them last time. Let's review them by reading them again.

Then in verse 5, we come to the first of our eight objectives. "Make very effort to add to your faith." *Add to* means "amplify, nourish, supplement with diligent effort."

Why do you think faith is the first of the eight objectives?
It is the beginning of our walk with God. Those who come to Him must believe He is and that He is a rewarder of those who diligently seek Him

First Corinthians 3:11 reinforces this same idea.

Not everyone has made Jesus the foundation of their life. What are some other foundations people might lay? Human wisdom, Hard work, self-reliance

What is wrong with those foundations? Why are they faulty? They are not God's way. There is a way that seems right to man, but its end is destruction

Many other Scriptures add to our understanding of this very important foundation of faith in Christ. Let's look at some of them together.

Acts 20:21
What does this say about establishing a foundation of faith? What two important steps are involved in coming to faith in Christ?
repentance toward God and faith toward our Lord Jesus Christ (circular?)
Testify - Rom 10:9-10

Romans 5:1
Another way to say *justified* is "made right with God." According to this verse, what comes after we have been made right with God through faith? Peace with God thru our Lord Jesus Christ

Workbook: *Insight Group*, Turning Point, P. O. Box 22127, Chattanooga, TN 37422-2127

Acts 13:38-39
What does this verse add to our understanding of faith in Christ?
Belief in Christ brings justification that could not come by the law

The Law could only point out sin—it could not forgive sin.

Acts 3:16
This verse identifies two other "benefits" that faith brings. What are they? Healing + perfect soundness (health)

Romans 1:17
What does this verse tell us about faith in Christ?
The righteous shall live by faith. We never arrive, but continue to live by faith

Romans 10:10, 17
What do these verses tell us about how a person comes to faith in Christ? Believe in your heart and be justified. Confess by mouth and you'll be saved. Faith comes from hearing and hearing through the Word of Christ

Once we come to Christ in faith, we begin to walk with God—a life of faith—on a daily basis. Back in the 2 Peter 1 passage, verse 5 says, "Make *every* effort to *add* to your faith." It implies, "Don't just settle for a thrilling conversion" and leave it at that. Instead, our saving faith is to mark the point where we begin the rewarding and demanding climb of the Christian life.

Let's take a look at some passages of Scripture that can help us better understand and experience this life of faith.

Philippians 4:13
Where does the strength come from? Him – Jesus. I can do all things through Him who strengthens me

Colossians 2:6-7
What guidance do these verses offer us about our life in Christ? We received in faith, walk in faith. Let your roots grow deep and your branches tall. Abound in thanksgiving

Hebrews 12:2
What advice do we find here for the times when we are feeling discouraged or tired or feel like we have failed? Look to Jesus, the founder + perfecter of our faith. He didn't go to the cross so that I could be defeated. Press on in faith and receive the victory He has for you.

Workbook: *Insight Group*, Turning Point, P. O. Box 22127, Chattanooga, TN 37422-2127

James 1:2-3

Why should we be glad for the hard times in our walk of faith?

They produce steadfastness, or endurance.

1 Peter 1:7

This expands on what James said. Why do the difficult times—the trials—come? They will result in praise, glory, and honor to Christ at the revelation of Christ

Romans 14:1a

What does the first half of this verse say about how we deal with other people in and outside of this group?

Welcome those weak in faith

(Don't quarrel over opinions.)

Application

Faith in Christ is the starting point for all the work God wants to do in our lives in the weeks ahead.

Here is the key question for each of us to consider: Is your faith in Jesus Christ the foundation of your life?

When have you been able to rest on (put trust in) that foundation?

How has your faith in Christ made a difference in the important areas of your life? In making important decisions? In dealing with problems? What about in the testing and hard times Peter and James wrote about?

Workbook: *Insight Group*, Turning Point, P. O. Box 22127, Chattanooga, TN 37422-2127

Session 3 The Trap

Personal Preparation: Getting Ready for Session Three

Meet With God

Personal Notes

Do not forget how important it is to spend time alone with God. Read from Psalm 31 and 1 Corinthians 6 and think about what God is saying to you. Invite God each day to work in your life.

Sharing Question

What is one quality from your parents that you wanted to re-create in your own life?

Faithfulness to each other. Hard work. Honesty
Made it across the finish line for God

Self-Awareness

We are going to talk about the "phases" of life-controlling problems. You will remember that a life-controlling problem is *anything* that masters our lives.

Because you have joined this group, you most likely agree with Paul, the writer of 1 Corinthians 6:12: "'Everything is permissible for me'—but not everything is beneficial. 'Everything is permissible for me'—but I will not be mastered by anything." To paraphrase that verse—Paul says, "Although 'anything goes,' I will not let any of them control me." Paul made a commitment.

Workbook: *Insight Group*, Turning Point, P. O. Box 22127, Chattanooga, TN 37422-2127

Every person has the potential of experiencing a life-controlling problem—no one is automatically exempt. And even though no one plans to be trapped by such a problem, it can happen without a person's even being aware.

Addictions and dependencies generally fall into three categories: *substance* addictions, *behavioral* addictions, and *relationship* (interaction) addictions. (There are other kinds of life-controlling problems and we may be talking about some of them later, but most fall into these three categories.)

1. **Substance addictions** (the use of substances taking control of our lives)
   - Drugs/chemicals
   - Food (eating disorders)
   - Alcohol
   - Other addictive substances

2. **Behavioral addictions** (the practice of behaviors taking control of our lives)
   - Gambling
   - Compulsive spending
   - Use of pornography/other sexual addictions
   - Love of money
   - Sports
   - Other addictive behavior

3. **Relationship (interaction) addictions** (You may have heard a relationship problem like this referred to as "co-dependency.") This is discussed in more detail in the Concerned Persons Group.

Everyone has the potential of experiencing one or more of these life-controlling problems. Maybe you find yourself already involved in an addiction or another problem behavior that has taken over your life.

Sometimes it is hard to identify a life-controlling problem. Here are some questions that may help in that process:

1. Is my behavior practiced in secret?
2. Can it meet the test of openness—or do I hide it from family and friends?
3. Does this behavior pull me away from my commitment to Christ?
4. Does it express Christian love?
5. Is this behavior used to escape feelings?
6. Does this behavior have a negative effect on myself or others?

These questions help us identify problems that have reached (or are in danger of reaching) the point of becoming life-controlling problems.

The next step is to look at the ways these behaviors and dependencies tend to progress in a person's life. Researchers have identified a pattern that follows some very predictable steps. We call it the Trap because it often snares its victims before they realize what is really happening. This week you had an opportunity to study the phases of life-controlling problems (which deal primarily with substance and behavioral addictions) as they are outlined in your workbook. We are going to look at those briefly to make sure we understand the progression.

Vernon E. Johnson, the founder and president emeritus of the Johnson Institute in Minneapolis, has observed (without trying to prove any theory) that "literally thousands of alcoholics, their families, and other people surrounding them . . . showed certain specific conditions with a remarkable consistency" (*I'll Quit Tomorrow*, p. 8).

Dr. Johnson uses a feeling chart to illustrate how alcoholism follows an emotional pattern. He identifies four phases: (1) learns mood swing, (2) seeks mood swing, (3) harmful dependency, (4) using to feel normal. Many of the observations made by Dr. Johnson and others can also be related to other types of dependencies although the terminology may differ.

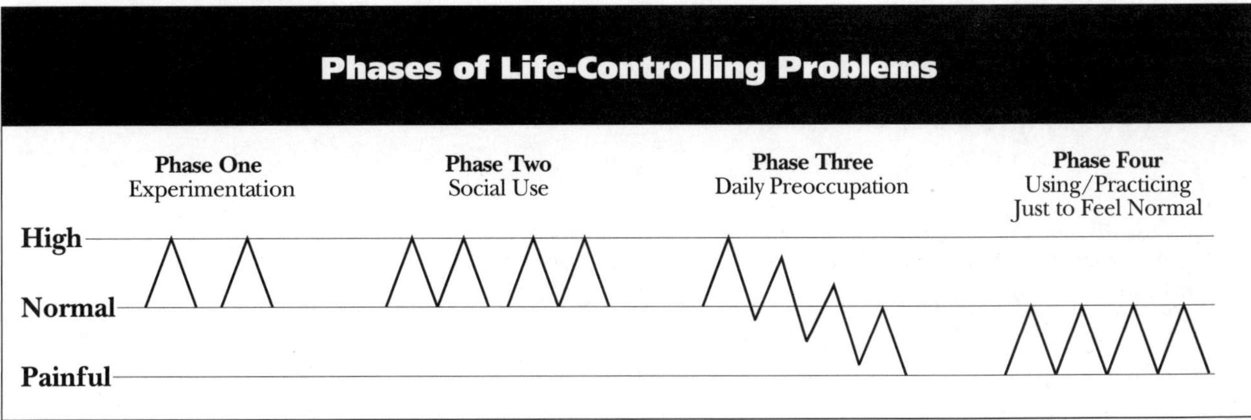

Phases of Life-Controlling Problems

Phase One: Experimentation

- I learn that experimenting with the substance/behavior makes me feel good.
- I don't really see any serious negative consequences.
- I learn to trust the substance/behavior to make me feel good or help me escape every time I use it or do it.
- I learn how to use the substance/behavior to make myself feel great.

Phase Two: Social Use

- I begin to use or practice more regularly.
- This behavior or substance becomes a part of my social life.
- I use or practice in times and places that are socially acceptable.
- Daily lifestyle choices begin to be affected by my focus on this substance/behavior.
- I make rules for myself about my use/practice to make me feel "safe."
- My use/behavior becomes a problem without warning.

Phase Three: Daily Preoccupation

- My use/practice becomes a harmful dependency.
- I begin to lose control over my use/practice.
- I violate my value system.
- I cannot block out the emotional pain.
- My lifestyle is centered on this compulsive behavior.
- Unresolved problems produce more stress and pain.
- I break my self-imposed "safe use/practice" rules.
- My life deteriorates in all areas, including health, spirituality, and relationships.

Phase Four: Using/Practicing Just to Feel Normal

- I lose touch with reality and experience delusions and paranoia.
- I may try to escape my problems by running away.
- I lose my desire to live.
- I have no desire for God—I am spiritually bankrupt.
- I lose control and dignity.
- My problems grow in a "snowball" effect.
- My family relationships are destroyed.

Let's think about Phase One. What situations or circumstances could cause a person to experiment with a potentially addictive substance or behavior?

Are there any warnings in the *Experimentation* phase and later in the *Social Use* phase that a serious problem is developing?

God is not in control – the substance/behavior is.

Why do some of us move past experimenting and social use and get more deeply entangled?

We ignore the Word and the Holy Spirit. The thrill or feeling "good" is more important than God and His Word.

In what phase do you think daily life begins to be noticeably affected? In phase I, one believes a lie – "There are no serious consequences." More apparent as the addiction progresses

While these four phases do not exactly represent every individual's experience, they have proven to be surprisingly accurate. After looking at these progressive phases of life-controlling problems, I'd like you to identify where you are right now.

Do you see yourself here?

Without identifying the person, can you think of someone in one of these phases? Explain. I know some trapped in homosexuality. Phase 3 or 4

These four phases form what we have called the Trap, and the most important fact for you to notice about the Trap is the way that it pulls a person deeper and deeper into a downward spiral.

It does not move in any sort of a positive direction or even in a neutral or straight line. It pulls us down.

Workbook: *Insight Group*, Turning Point, P. O. Box 22127, Chattanooga, TN 37422-2127

What are some of the ways the Trap pulls us down? What areas of life are affected in a seriously negative way?

Pulls one away from God – leads to spiritual bankruptcy
Family relationships are destroyed
Can lead to other problems because one is away from God

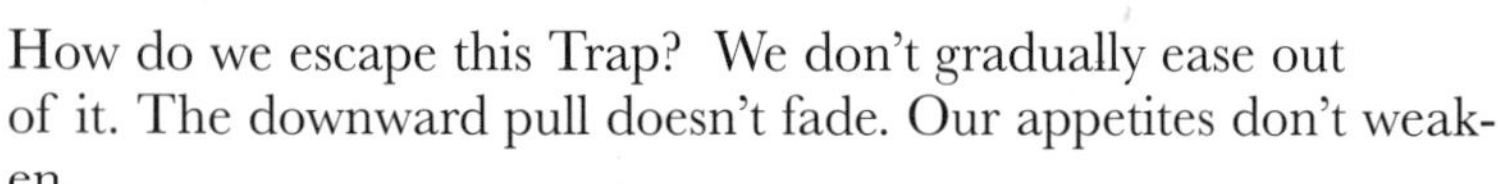

Spiritual Awareness: Goodness

How do we escape this Trap? We don't gradually ease out of it. The downward pull doesn't fade. Our appetites don't weaken.

The only way to escape the Trap is to come to a turning point where we *resolve* to live a life that is free of the behavior or dependence or whatever masters us.

We find this same idea in 2 Peter 1:3-4. We need Gods (divine) power to break the spiral. Claim his great & precious promises, by which we can partake the Divine Nature & escape the corruption in the world

In verse 5 we read, "For this very reason, make every effort to add to your faith goodness." Goodness is virtue or moral excellence. It involves firm resolution—an active choice—for moral excellence. The word *goodness* implies a firm commitment to shun corruption.

The performance of goodness may not always be there, but God puts the want-to there. We have to cultivate that desire and put it into action.

Later
Phil 2:13 For it is God who works in you, both to will and to work for his good pleasure

We want to look at some other verses that can help us understand what goodness means.

Phil. 2:12-13

Workbook: *Insight Group*, Turning Point, P. O. Box 22127, Chattanooga, TN 37422-2127

Romans 8:12-13
Those of us who have struggled with life-controlling problems know all about "the sinful nature." And if we're caught in the trap of addiction or dependence, we've made the mistake of living "according to" our sinful nature.

These verses offer both a warning and a hope. Can you find each in verse 13? Live according to the flesh, you will die (spiritually). But if you put to death the deeds of the body by the Spirit, you will live

Notice where the strength and the power come from—"by the Spirit." It does not say "by yourself."

What will be the result of obeying the Holy Spirit?
Life - abundant life

Ephesians 2:1-3
What do these verses say about a person who is dead in sin? How does following the desires and thoughts of the sinful nature affect a person's life? He is following Satan, living for him, doing his bidding. Makes Satan's nature ours. Contrast with having the divine nature

Romans 8:11
What does this say about the power the Holy Spirit brings to our life and to our struggle with our sinful nature? God will give life to our mortal bodies through the Spirit who dwells in us.

Philippians 2:12-13
When we feel like the fight against our sinful nature is impossible, this verse has some encouragement for us. What is it? God gives us the will & the ability to do His good pleasure

Psalm 37:5-6
What do these verses say about the relationship between righteousness (or goodness) and commitment? Commit your way to the Lord and He will act. He will bring forth our righteousness and justice

These verses from the Psalms also talk about God's commitment to us. We commit and put our trust in Him—and He will make our light "shine like the dawn."

Philippians 4:8
Why do you think this verse talks about our thinking? As a man thinks in his heart, so is he Prov. 23:7

Workbook: *Insight Group*, Turning Point, P. O. Box 22127, Chattanooga, TN 37422-2127

What sort of a "test" can we formulate from this verse that will warn us when our thoughts might be leading us into trouble?

Job 31:1
Job saw right to the heart of his problem. His eyes were the "gate" that could allow lustful thoughts. Can you think of an active choice you could make to avoid the "gate" that allows a life-controlling problem into your life? Is there a specific covenant you can make with yourself like Job did? Maybe it would mean saying to your feet, "Don't walk to that place"; or you may need to talk to your hands or your mouth or your eyes—as Job did.

Daniel 1:8
This verse carries a similar idea as the one from Job. What is the key word here?

1 Corinthians 16:13
Why would this be a good verse to memorize?

Application

Several important ideas stand out from these verses:

1. We are fighting an enemy inside ourselves—our own sinful nature.

2. That enemy wants to lead us to death.

3. The only way to overcome this enemy (and to escape from the trap that holds us) is to live a life of faith in Christ and be led by His Spirit. *Goodness* does not just happen in our lives—goodness grows out of our relationship with Jesus Christ.

4. Good news! We are not alone in the struggle. God gives us the strength to carry it out! All the help we will need is generously available to us.

Once we have come to Christ in saving faith, His Spirit in us can provide all the energy we need to stand firm in our commitment. That same Spirit is able to guide us, step by step, out of the patterns that hold us. We need only to listen, be willing to obey, and stay in fellowship with believers.

Workbook: *Insight Group*, Turning Point, P. O. Box 22127, Chattanooga, TN 37422-2127

Which of these areas is hardest for you to accept and act on?

- Recognizing and understanding the fight against our own sin natures.
- Making a firm resolution to shun corruption.
- Relying on the Holy Spirit for guidance and strength. Key to others

What commitment have you made to add goodness to your faith?

Workbook: *Insight Group*, Turning Point, P. O. Box 22127, Chattanooga, TN 37422-2127

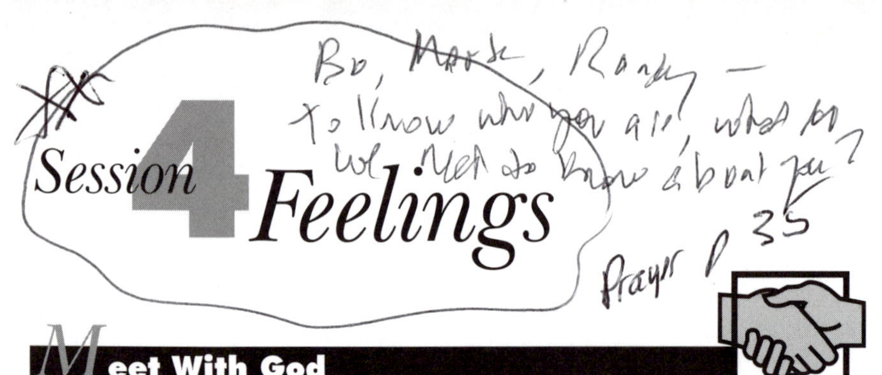

Session 4 Feelings

Personal Preparation: Getting Ready for Session Four

Meet With God

Personal Notes

Have you found a regular time and place to meet with God each day? Nothing will help you stand firm in your commitment to Christ and to moral excellence like a daily time in God's word and in prayer.

Read Psalms 32 and 91 for some practical wisdom. In your prayer time, ask God to give you special insight into your feelings and emotions this week.

Sharing Question

What is one part of your life that you enjoy and one part that is difficult for you?

Self-Awareness

Our topic this time is *feelings* and the importance of knowing our true feelings and being able to express them.

Just about every person alive has some degree of trouble with this, but it is an especially difficult area for those who struggle with life-controlling problems. We have a hard time recognizing and admitting our true feelings, so we are going to spend some time now talking about feelings and emotions and how we can be more honest with ourselves and with others about what is going on inside us. We are going to look at why it is so important for us to understand our feelings and share them with others.

All through the Bible, we find examples and encouragement that point us toward the importance of knowing our feelings and not keeping our feelings hidden inside. Jesus had emotions, and He expressed them. He cried. He got angry. He was sad. Hebrews tells

Workbook: *Insight Group*, Turning Point, P. O. Box 22127, Chattanooga, TN 37422-2127

us that Jesus carried the experience of human feelings with Him to His place at the right hand of God (Hebrews 4:15). He understands and sympathizes with our feelings.

We are going to start by looking at why sharing our feelings is so important. These are just some of the problems hidden feelings (or frozen or numb feelings) can cause:

1. **When we do not recognize our true feelings, we never deal with what is really bothering us.** When we avoid being honest about our real feelings, problems do not get solved and usually get worse as they are bottled up.

2. **Hiding our true feelings keeps us from being known.** We hide how we feel behind a defense to keep our real self from showing through. We may be fearful or angry or sad inside, but we hide those feelings by joking or acting superior or being silent or employing some other defense.

   There are dozens of ways we cover up our true feelings, and we will be talking about those defenses in our next session, but for now let me just say that the biggest problem with defenses is that they keep us isolated behind a false shell. And if we continue to "live a lie," eventually we can come to the place where we believe it ourselves—when even we do not really know who we are. That is called *delusion.* Delusion is a false belief system.

3. **Hidden (unexpressed or frozen) feelings strengthen the bondage of life-controlling problems.** Addictions and dependencies feed on hidden feelings, and those unknown and unspoken feelings intensify our bondage to these problems that control us. Knowing how you feel and being able to express those feelings is a key to breaking out of life-controlling problems.

In your preparation for this session, you will come across a list of feelings on page 30 of your workbook. It does not include every possible human emotion, but it is a good start.

I hope you are able to use that list to become more aware of your own feelings.

Something that is important to remember about those feelings that are *hard* to express is that by keeping them inside, they actually grow stronger. But you will probably find—as others have—that by leveling (by being honest) about what you are feeling, you lessen its power. Keeping a feeling secret—like fear—actually increases its power.

Workbook: *Insight Group*, Turning Point, P. O. Box 22127, Chattanooga, TN 37422-2127

Feelings Checklist

- ❑ accepted
- ❑ afraid
- ❑ angry
- ❑ anxious
- ❑ attractive
- ❑ beaten
- ❑ brave
- ❑ calm
- ❑ cheated
- ❑ cheerful
- ❑ confident
- ❑ confused
- ❑ cowardly
- ❑ cruel
- ❑ defeated
- ❑ depressed
- ❑ desperate
- ❑ different
- ❑ disappointed
- ❑ embarrassed
- ❑ excited
- ❑ fearful
- ❑ friendless
- ❑ frustrated
- ❑ gentle
- ❑ grateful
- ❑ guilty
- ❑ happy
- ❑ hateful
- ❑ hopeless
- ❑ hurt
- ❑ hypocritical
- ❑ ignored
- ❑ impatient
- ❑ independent
- ❑ inferior
- ❑ insecure
- ❑ jealous
- ❑ judged
- ❑ like a loser
- ❑ lonely
- ❑ loved
- ❑ loving
- ❑ loyal
- ❑ macho
- ❑ misunderstood
- ❑ needy
- ❑ neglected
- ❑ out of touch
- ❑ overlooked
- ❑ persecuted
- ❑ phony
- ❑ preoccupied
- ❑ proud
- ❑ quiet
- ❑ rejected
- ❑ repulsive
- ❑ sad
- ❑ secure
- ❑ shy
- ❑ silly
- ❑ sorry for myself
- ❑ stupid
- ❑ suicidal
- ❑ superior
- ❑ supported
- ❑ suspicious
- ❑ touchy
- ❑ ugly
- ❑ upbeat
- ❑ uptight
- ❑ useless
- ❑ valuable
- ❑ violent
- ❑ weak

Basic Human Feelings

Within the feelings checklist are some of the *most basic* human emotions. We all experience them at one time or another. Of all the feelings you can experience, these are important ones to recognize and express. They are:

- **Anger**—feeling hostile, indignant, or exasperated
- **Sadness**—being sorrowful and unhappy
- **Fear**—feeling anxious or apprehensive
- **Guilt**—being regretfully aware of having done wrong
- **Shame**—feeling embarrassment or disgrace
- **Gladness**—feeling happiness or joy

Workbook: *Insight Group*, Turning Point, P. O. Box 22127, Chattanooga, TN 37422-2127

Think about the times you have experienced these feelings. Choose one of the feelings that you can relate to a particular event or experience in your life. Describe.

Sadness + fear: learned Jim had throat cancer - being kept from family - quit taking all meds, had not been out of the house for 2 years, and refused hospice. Decided to go see him and take any family who wanted to go. Fear - he wouldn't see me or would die before I saw him. God gave us a great visit and a chance to witness

The Johari Window

Another illustration that helps us understand why we may hide our feelings—even from ourselves—is the Johari Window. When a person violates God's law, they should feel guilty and ashamed; and the pain should bring them back to the truth.

If a person denies the truth and excuses this behavior, they will bury these emotions. As this continues, a person does not see the truth about themselves and becomes unfeeling. The Apostle Paul speaks to this process in Ephesians 4:17-19. "Who, being past feeling, have given themselves over..." (v. 19, KJV).

The Johari Window	
1: OPEN Known to me and openly shared with others.	**2: SECRET** What I know and choose to hide from others.
3: BLIND What others know about me but I cannot see for myself.	**4: SUBCONSCIOUS** The part of me that is hidden to all.

Joseph Luft in Group Processes *describes the origin of the Johari Window. Dr. Harrington V. Ingham of the University of California at Los Angeles and Joseph Luft developed it during a summer laboratory in the 1950s. Johari is pronounced as a combination of the names Joe and Harry—the developers' names (57).*

Think about yourself in terms of this illustration—particularly windowpane three. Could you be blind to areas of your life that should be dealt with honestly? Explain.

One of the helping roles this group (and other caring friends in the body of Christ) can play in your life is to provide the feedback you need in order to see into your "blind" area. It is very difficult for us to see ourselves the way we really are, and we can help each other through loving—but honest—confrontation. We can also pray that the Holy Spirit will open our eyes to the truth about ourselves.

When we talk about *defenses* in our next session, we will be looking at that blind area and how our life-controlling problems are tied to living too much in a distorted reality of our own making. When we come to actually believe that false reality, we call it *delusion*.

As we grow in our awareness of our true feelings—when we stop hiding how we really feel, then we can begin to deal with the real issues in our lives.

Some of our hidden feelings simply need to be shared so we can better understand ourselves. But some of the feelings we will discuss—like resentment, lust, jealousy, or envy—are sinful; and those feelings need to be confessed and made right with God.

Your past has been greatly influenced by your feelings—both those you have acknowledged and those that remain hidden. But this can be a *turning point* in your life as you begin to act—not on the basis of your feelings which can be flawed but based on your growing knowledge of Jesus Christ and who you are in Him.

You will not be able to "fix" all your feelings immediately—that is really a process, but you can begin right now to establish *right thinking* and *right behavior.* When you take those two important steps, then *right feelings* will follow.

During our bible study time, we are going to talk about that right thinking that is based on knowledge and not on feelings.

Spiritual Awareness: Knowledge

Once again we will turn to 2 Peter1:5. "For this very reason, make every effort to add to your faith goodness [you remember that goodness is moral excellence]; and [add] to [your] goodness, *knowledge*."

Knowledge here is not just an accumulation of facts but a gaining of practical understanding. We are challenged to a growing knowledge of Jesus Christ.

Rather than letting our actions be determined by our feelings (which can delude us), we need to base our actions on what is certain and true. It is knowledge that leads to right decisions and right actions in the sight of God.

Before we leave 2 Peter 1, look back at verse 2.

What can knowledge of God and Jesus Christ do for us?

How often do *feelings* bring you grace and peace?

We need to begin to live based on our knowledge of who we are through faith in Jesus Christ. To get our thinking moving along those lines, we are going to look at some verses that will remind us of who we are in Jesus.

Ephesians 1:7
What do we have in Jesus Christ?

How does this contrast with what our feelings might be telling us about ourselves?

Philippians 4:13
What message do we get from this verse that is different from what we often feel?

What do our feelings often say?

Philippians 1:6
Put this verse into a slogan or a promise you can carry with you for the times when encouragement is needed.

How is God doing a "good thing" in your life? What kind of work is He doing?

John 16:13 and Psalm 32:8
What knowledge do these verses offer us for the times when our feelings might be telling us we are alone or when we are feeling unsure of what to do?

Workbook: *Insight Group*, Turning Point, P. O. Box 22127, Chattanooga, TN 37422-2127

Psalm 91:1-6
When you have the time, read the rest of this psalm and meditate on all the images of safety and security you will find there. This is a great place to come when feelings of fear threaten you.

Verse 4 shows a picture of being sheltered under protective wings.

Have you ever experienced those protective wings?

Romans 8:37
Once we come to Christ in faith, we have a whole new identity.

Under the authority of this verse, what new label can we attach to ourselves?

Application

Through these Bible verses, we have seen a picture of our new identity in Jesus Christ:

- We are redeemed—paid for at great cost.
- We are forgiven—clean; our sin has been forgotten.
- We are strong and capable—we can do everything through Christ.
- We are conquerors—overcomers.

What does this new identity in Christ mean to you personally?

What would change in your life if you stopped making choices based on your feelings and started living and making decisions based on who you are in Christ?

What struggles can you overcome because of who you are in Christ?

Workbook: *Insight Group*, Turning Point, P. O. Box 22127, Chattanooga, TN 37422-2127

Session 5

Defenses and Isolation

Meet With God

One of the most important disciplines of the Christian life is to find time each day to get alone with God. We hope you are continuing to build that time into your daily schedule. As you pray this week ask God to give you a sensitivity to any walls of defenses you may be building into your life. You will find it helpful to read Romans 8 and 12.

Rom 12:2 Be in the world and be conformed or in the Word and be transformed. Word renews our minds = see as God sees.

Personal Preparation: Getting Ready for Session Five

Thank God for members
What He has been doing in our lives
Break down walls between each other
ask God

Personal Notes

Rom 8:6 - Set mind on flesh = death. Set mind on Spirit = life & peace

Sharing Question

What is your favorite spot in your home or garden, and why? Deck or patio - sensing nature brings me close to God (Deer [illegible])

Self-Awareness

You remember that in our last session we talked about how we often have a hard time recognizing and admitting what we really feel.

Of course, this sharing of feelings is much more than a one-week project. It is an ongoing process as we learn to be honest with ourselves and with others about our feelings.

It is human nature to build defenses to hide our feeling

Workbook: *Insight Group*, Turning Point, P. O. Box 22127, Chattanooga, TN 37422-2127

We also looked at some of the serious problems that hidden feelings can cause, and the dangers of being "blind" to our own feelings. *Denial* is another word we can use to talk about the condition of being blinded to our own feelings.

In his book, *Sin—Overcoming the Deadly Addiction,* Keith Miller paints a picture that can help us better understand the danger of hidden feelings and denial. He writes:

> Our feelings constitute a wonderful "warning system" that tells us when we need to focus on a certain danger area in our lives or something that needs our love and attention.
>
> But when we are in denial, we bury these feelings—push them into our unconscious like pushing giant beach balls under water. When a feeling does get loose it comes up with exaggerated force "at an angle" and may hurt someone—like a beach ball that has been pushed far under water and finally pops to the surface (pg 101).

If you have ever tried to hold an inflated toy under water, you know what hard work that can be. But we work *even harder* to keep our true feelings out of view. We build walls around our real selves and around the stronghold (life-controlling problem). These walls cause us to:

1. Isolate ourselves from other people. Proverbs 18:1 (NKJV) points out the danger: "A man who isolates himself seeks his own desire; He rages against all wise judgment."

2. Isolate ourselves from God.

3. Hide from the truth about a growing or full-blown dependency or addiction.

Defenses

These walls we build are called "defenses," and I would like us to talk about some commonly used defenses and think about which ones we may be using. But first we need to understand that defenses are not usually selected or planned. We do not consciously think, "I'm going to hide myself behind such-and-such defense."

Defenses We All Use to Some Extent

Read thru and mark three or so.
Anyone want to share?

- Rationalization: "It's not my fault." "We're living in a new age." "Everybody's doing it."
- ✓ Humor (joking, grinning, laughing): "Reminds me of a funny story."
- Blaming, accusing: First used by Adam and Eve. He blames her; she blames the serpent (Genesis 3:12-13).
- Denying: Blind to the truth about self, "I do not...." (Genesis 4:9; John 18:15-27).
- Justifying: "You don't understand the pressure I'm under."
- Intellectualizing: "In my reading I have found...."
- Debating, arguing: "That's one way of looking at it."
- Minimizing: "What I did isn't so bad."
- Evading, dodging: "You must be talking about someone else."
- ✓ Withdrawing: "I'm going for a walk."
- Silence: "I don't want to talk about this."
- Shouting, intimidating: "Shut up!"
- Threatening: "If you mention this again, I will...."
- Glaring: Staring you down.
- Smiling: This false happiness covers up real sadness or pain.
- ✓ Complying: "Whatever you say."
- Playing dumb: "I don't know how I...."
- Spiritualizing: "God told me to...."

Now read through the list again and write down some of the defenses you may have used. Make a note of any feeling you may have hidden behind.

Defense	**The Way I Really Feel**
humor	attacked - for what I believe
withdraw	disappointed - for lack of support
complying	defeated - not went to other way

Workbook: *Insight Group*, Turning Point, P. O. Box 22127, Chattanooga, TN 37422-2127

Leveling

We have been focusing on defenses this session; but before we move on to our Spiritual Awareness time, I want to change direction for just a minute to talk about something called leveling. To remove one brick at a time from the walls of our defenses, it is important to learn to level.

1. Leveling about our feelings is openly admitting them.
2. To level is to respond openly. Examples: With God (Luke 18:10-14), with self (Romans 12:3), and with others (2 Samuel 12:13).
3. We level when we take the risk of being known by spontaneously reporting our feelings.

Our personal goal should be to replace *isolation* with *sharing*.

What would be the hardest part for you in making that change?

We level when we tell someone we are hurt—or afraid—or angry. Using these particular feelings as an example is useful for three reasons:

1. Anger bottled up or fear kept hidden seems to lead to more relapses in recovery from addictions and dependencies than any other feelings.
2. Anger and fear are two of the most difficult feelings to express.
3. Anger and fear—if not dealt with—result in isolation.

I would encourage you—some time in the days ahead—to ask God to give you insight into any anger that is bottled up inside, any fears you are hiding, or any signs of isolation in your life. Go back over the information in your workbook and see if you have some old anger or hidden fears to deal with and resolve.

Briefly go over the development of emotional problems. Notice the recovery statement for fear and anger and move on.

Workbook: *Insight Group*, Turning Point, P. O. Box 22127, Chattanooga, TN 37422-2127

Anger and Fear

Two of the hardest feelings to admit are fear and anger. They are also two of the most common emotional trouble spots. Of course, not everyone lives with hidden fear or anger, but it is still worthwhile to understand these powerful emotions.

Read through the phases of these feeling-caused problems and ask yourself if there is any fear or anger in your life that needs to be acknowledged and dealt with.

Development of Emotional Problems Related to Fear

By Dr. Raymond Brock

Used by permission

Phase 1: Stress

Any stressor in life that becomes overwhelming—people, places, or things—creates stress. This could be a job, a difficult person, or some other pressure point.

Phase 2: Anxiety

A reaction to the person, circumstance, or situation that causes our stress produces anxiety.

Phase 3: Avoidance

- Avoid confrontation with the source of our stress (i.e., call in sick to work, avoid family gatherings or other contact with difficult person, etc.).
- Bitterness begins to grow.
- Unforgiveness is used as an avoidance technique.
- Avoiding the real issue isolates an individual and keeps them alone in fear and stress.

Phase 4: Reinforcement

- The more the problem is avoided, the harder it becomes to *ever* deal with the anxiety or the source of stress.
- The problem persists because it is not confronted realistically.

Recovery: Instead of avoiding the issue, deal with the anxiety and reverse the cycle of fear. The source of stress must be confronted rather than avoided. That confrontation is the only way the stress and anxiety can be resolved.

Workbook: *Insight Group*, Turning Point, P. O. Box 22127, Chattanooga, TN 37422-2127

Development of Emotional Problems Related to Anger

By Dr. Raymond Brock

Used by permission

Phase 1: Hurt

Hurt is created when feelings are bruised from personal slight or disappointment.

Phase 2: Frustration

The feeling that comes when life tells you NO! is frustration

Phase 3: Fear

The feeling that comes with loss of control and anticipation of reprisal is fear.

Phase 4: Anger

Feelings of hurt that are complicated by frustration and fear create anger.

Phase 5: Wrath

Anger that has "brewed overnight" and gets stronger and grows into bitterness and unforgiveness is wrath.

Phase 6: Hostility

Anger collected and aggressive becomes hostility.

Phase 7: Hate

Bottled-up hostility which may be turned inward in depression or grow to the point of exploding into violence directed at one's self or toward the person or group that is blamed for the original hurt is hate.

Recovery: To deal with anger, go back to the hurt, acknowledge the hurt, and take responsibility for your part and forgive the other person for their part.

Have you witnessed these effects in anyone's life? Describe.

In our Spiritual Awareness time today, our subject is *self-control*. The Bible has a great deal to say on this subject, and we will be looking at a number of verses that talk about self-control. But first I want to discuss a *false* sense of self-control you may have experienced.

When we isolate ourselves behind walls and defenses, we have a sense that we are in control:

- We are holding our feelings "under control." (Remember the beach balls?)
- We are keeping other people at a "safe" distance.

- We may have the secrets of our (developing) addictions and dependencies well-hidden and feel as if they are under control.
- We may have developed some "safe" rules related to our problem substance or behavior that feed this false sense that we are in control of the situation.

In fact, we may be seeing a distorted reality—a delusion, and our false sense of self-control can blow up at any time.

In our misguided attempts to get our lives under control, what we actually have done is:

- Pushed away the people who really care about us—the ones who could help us.
- Allowed hidden and suppressed feelings to fester and ferment and grow.
- Become slaves—in bondage to a mastering problem that wants to take over more and more of our lives.

Spiritual Awareness: Self-Control

That false kind of "self-control" ends in depression and despair. But in the next few minutes, we are going to talk about the *true* self-control we read about in 2 Peter 1. Let's read together starting at verse 3.

A meaningful definition of self-control is "mastery of appetites," but that mastery of our appetites runs counter to the desires of the flesh. Our sin nature pushes us toward self-indulgence, but God's Word says that our lives in Christ should be characterized by *self-control.* Self-control results from Spirit control

What are some of the differences between self-indulgence and self-control? Do I do what I want or what God wants?

Workbook: *Insight Group*, Turning Point, P. O. Box 22127, Chattanooga, TN 37422-2127

What are some of the ways our feelings and sin nature can push us toward self-indulgence? What are some of the wrong messages our feelings tell us?

It will not hurt. You have been doing better – you deserve to reward yourself

---

Second Peter tells us that self-control grows out of knowledge. When we start living and choosing and acting on the basis of what we *know* about who we are in Christ—and what we *know* about all the strength and guidance and wisdom God has promised to provide, then we can begin to practice *true* self-control.

How can a life based on the knowledge of who we are in Christ lead us to self-control?

We are His child – I have His nature in me. I am His witness. Others' eternal state depends on my witness

What kind of right thinking comes out of that knowledge that enables us to take control back from the problems that master us?

God never leaves me nor forsakes me. He has all power and all wisdom. Being used of God is a fulfilling, rewarding possibility

---

The Bible has a great deal to say about the importance of self-control and how we can practice self-control in our lives.

Before we go on to some of these other verses, let's look at an important phrase in 2 Peter 1:5. It says to "make every effort." Self-control involves a great deal of effort—it is hard work. You have already made an effort to attend our sessions together and to do the homework each week, and I commend you for your hard work and your faithfulness. Just keep in mind that this whole area of self-control involves a lot of *our* effort along with a lot of help from God.

Make the effort and God will make it happen

These first verses talk about *right thinking* and changes that come from the inside out.

Romans 12:1-2
What does this verse say about right thinking?

Right thinking – seeing as God sees – will transform us

Listen to this definition of renew: "To make like new. Renew implies so extensive a remaking that what had become faded and disintegrated is now like new."

Isn't it exciting to think that God is able to do all that for a mind that has been deadened by sin?

How do you think God wants to work in the mind of a person who is mastered by a life-controlling problem?

He wants to transform us

---

2 Corinthians 10:5b

There are many good ideas in this passage, but we want to focus on a phrase in the second part of this verse: "We take captive every thought to make it obedient to Christ."

How can we exercise self-control in our thoughts? Think on things pure, lovely, of a good report. Recite or quote a scripture or sing a chorus to change the direction of our thoughts

Why is this important?

As a person thinks in their heart, so are they

These next two verses also talk about how right thinking helps us practice self-control.

1 Thessalonians 5:6

What do you need to be alert for? Don't be spiritually asleep, but awake and sober

---

1 Peter 5:8

How does Satan use our life-controlling problems to devour us?

Attention, time and thoughts spent on them are not only wasted, they destroy us if they are not overcome

---

1 Peter 1:13

This verse says we should not only be alert, but we should also think ahead. How can we "prepare our minds" for action? Pray the Holy Spirit will help us guard our hearts and minds. Determine what we should do when those thoughts come

---

Psalm 119:11

What are some of the ways that knowing God's Word can help us master our appetites? Knowing Satan's devices. Knowing our weakness. Quoting the Word – as Jesus did – when temptations come

Workbook: *Insight Group*, Turning Point, P. O. Box 22127, Chattanooga, TN 37422-2127

Colossians 3:5-10
This passage identifies many different sins of the flesh. It is interesting to realize that the problems people struggled with back in Bible times are still with us today. That is because we still have the same sin nature that fights for control in our lives.

Looking at these verses, what are the practices from your old self that you struggle with?

Romans 8:13
What does it mean to "live according to the flesh" (NKJV)?

This verse tells us that if we live according to the sinful nature—live to please the flesh, then we will die spiritually. But this verse also has a positive message. What is it?

Left to ourselves, we are not strong enough to discipline our passions. Anyone who has struggled against a life-controlling problem and lost a battle knows that to be true.

Of course, we are to "make every effort" to add to our knowledge self-control, and these verses have pointed out some of the important work we need to do.

But ultimately, true self-control comes through submission to Jesus Christ. When we turn ourselves over to His control and submit to His will for us each day, then we can find the strength to master our appetites and overcome life-controlling problems.

Here is another passage to help us understand further.

Galatians 5:22-24
Self-control is identified as a "fruit of the Spirit." How can we have this fruit in our lives?

Titus 2:11-12
When you bring the whole idea of self-control and our battle with our sin nature down to the level of everyday living, it really comes down to this issue: When are we able to say no? Can anyone relate a time when the grace of God has enabled you to say no? It may have been in something that seemed small, but practicing self-control is a series of relatively small decisions that come together to make up the patterns of our lives.

Workbook: *Insight Group*, Turning Point, P. O. Box 22127, Chattanooga, TN 37422-2127

Application

I am sure this is not the first time you have heard about self-control, but I hope our study has added to your understanding of how it is *possible* for us to:

- Put to death the sins of the body.
- Be transformed by the renewing of our mind.
- Take captive every thought and make it obedient to Christ.
- Be alert and self-controlled.
- Prepare our minds for action and be self-controlled.
- Hide God's Word in our hearts that we might not sin against God.
- Rely on the Holy Spirit in us for the strength we need.
- Say no—by God's grace—to the ungodly passions that want to master us.

Let's bring this down to a personal level and talk about how we are dealing with this issue of self-control. What are you finding to be the most difficult part of practicing self-control? When sharing the gospel, it is not what others think of me, it is what God thinks

What is God teaching you in this area?

Ask "What does God think?" That is renewing my mind

Practicing true self-control begins in our minds. It begins with *right thinking* that leads to *right actions*. As you go through this week, let God's Spirit in you make you sensitive to wrong thoughts. Let Him give you the strength to say no to ungodliness and worldly passions.

Session 6 Symptoms

Personal Preparation: Getting Ready for Session Six

Meet With God

Personal Notes

In your personal prayer time this week, ask God to help you be honest with yourself and with other people He wants to help us break down the walls that surround us. Read Joshua 6 for a story about how God is able to break down walls.

march around 1 day. 7th day march around 7 times, priests 7 trumpets will blow trumpets. when they make a long blast, the people will shout → walls will fall flat

Hebrews 4:12-16 reminds us how important it is for us to spend time each day in Bible study and prayer. Pray for other group members as God brings them to your mind.

Word is living, active, sharper than any two-edged sword, piercing to the division of soul and of spirit, of joints and of marrow and discerning the thoughts & intents of the heart
Jesus sympathizes with our weaknesses
Let us with confidence draw near to the throne of grace that we may receive mercy and find grace to help in time of need.

Sharing Question

When you have some free time to yourself, what do you like to do?

Organize family photos & videos
walk & enjoy out of doors
Work Sudoku puzzles

Self-Awareness

This session brings attention to the symptoms that often accompany life-controlling problems. Having discussed denial, delusion, and feelings in previous sessions, you may now see yourself more clearly and relate to one or more of these signs.

Our focus will be perseverance.

Workbook: *Insight Group*, Turning Point, P. O. Box 22127, Chattanooga, TN 37422-2127

For just a few minutes, think about your life as a long car trip. It started at birth. Of course, *your parents* drove for quite a few years; but then *you* took over the steering wheel.

You did fine for a while, but lately you are beginning to wonder about the direction you are going. You wonder exactly where you are right now and whether or not you should even be visiting this particular region.

One way to identify your location is to start (if you have not already) reading the signs along the side of the road. They indicate what highway you are following, in what direction you are headed, and what destination you would like to reach.

Of course, this picture has its limitations; but I believe it can help us understand where we may be going with a life-controlling problem or the development of one. What are the road signs we should be noticing, and just where are we headed?

Are we headed for heaven?
" " " towards a deeper relationship with Christ?
" " " for a place where we can do His will?
" " " " " " " " be used 2 Him?
" " Can we help others — nonbeliever + believers?

We are going to go through the list of symptoms that follow the typical progression of a life-controlling problem. There are some questions I would like for us to think about as we move through the list:

- What are the road signs—or symptoms—that we should be aware of that warn of a life-controlling problem?
- What do these signs and symptoms tell us about how far our life-controlling problem has come in its attempts to master our lives?
- How can we be more aware of these signs, and how can we be warned by them?

As we go through this list, resist the tendency to deny any signs or symptoms that might be present in your life. Just because we may talk about examples that do not specifically fit your situation, ask God to help you to honestly see how each one might apply to your life.

Symptoms of Life-Controlling Problems

A growing *anticipation* of behavioral practice or substance use leads to preoccupation. This usually grows out of the social phase discussed in Session 3.

Preoccupation

1. The mind is increasingly filled with thoughts of the substance or behavior.

2. Vacation times and other recreation is planned around substance or behavior.

3. In times of boredom, the mind seeks the stimulation of thinking about the substance or behavior.

4. There is a growing need for the substance/behavior in times of stress.

Substance may be used in an attempt to prevent stress; i.e., "This is going to be a long, hard day. I'd better take a pill," or "I'll need my medication."

5. Even as the substance or behavior takes over the thought life, the individual may put on the face of normalcy. Other people may not know.

Growing Rigidity in Lifestyle

1. Rituals develop that lead to use/behavior in small, seemingly innocent steps.

2. Frustration and anger occur when the ritual is interrupted or when someone interferes with the ritual.

3. Particular times of the day are set aside for use or practice.

4. Self-imposed rules are adjusted or ignored as the need grows.

5. Social events and free-time activities are limited to those which accommodate the practice or usage.

Loss of Control

1. All areas of the lifestyle are structured to serve and support the life-controlling problem.

2. The use or practice is no longer limited to set times of the day.

Workbook: *Insight Group*, Turning Point, P. O. Box 22127, Chattanooga, TN 37422-2127

3. There are repeated harmful consequences resulting from the life-controlling problem; but even so, the use or behavior cannot stop.

Go back to our picture of the car trip for a moment. Think about some of the signs you have passed—some of the indicators that could warn you of a growing problem.

Let's look at these symptoms or road signs once again and talk about where we can see ourselves and our own experiences in them.

I may say God is first, but times of worship are ignored, God's people are down on the list, reading the Word and prayer have lower priority. Time with others, who don't share my addiction, is not important.
Am I headed the correct way?

Preoccupation

We will start with this area of preoccupation. During times when there is not much else going on, do you find yourself *thinking about* and planning for a time when you will be able to use or practice?

Have you ever found yourself planning a vacation or leisure time on the basis of how it would serve the needs of your life-controlling problem (i.e., centered around drinking or gambling)?

Rituals and Rigidity

Now let's think about the rituals and other structures that start to develop around our use or practice. You had some opportunity during your preparation time this week to start thinking about some of the things you do every day in terms of this idea of rituals. Have you had any success in identifying some rituals in your life? They may be hard to spot because they can be normal and seemingly harmless actions that are only significant in the way they lead you into use or practice, but they can lead into hard-set rules.

We may try to fool ourselves into believing that some of these rituals are actually good for us because they appear to "limit" our use or practice to certain times of the day or because they "help" to control us within certain "safe" limits. In fact, they are far from harmless as they begin—step by step—to take over the shape and structure of our lives. We start letting our problem with this substance or behavior shape our schedule and take charge of our free time. Who will my friends be? (Those who will not interfere with my use/practice.) When will I go to sleep? (After I slip in one last use/practice while the rest of the family is in bed.) What route will I drive home from work? (The one that lets me stop and maintain my supply.)

These are limited examples, but I think they can give us an idea of how these seemingly harmless rituals can begin to control our lives. Can you tell us some of the rituals you have adopted to serve your life-controlling problem? In what ways have you made plans to accommodate and make room for this use or behavior?

What rules had you made for yourself concerning your use/practice that you later broke?

Loss of Control

Let's move on to the symptoms that indicate when—for the most part—control has passed from us to a life-controlling problem.

One evidence of loss of control is when a person's lifestyle is determined by use or practice. In an earlier phase, use or practice was planned around daily routines and obligations, but this is different. Now, use or practice is any time, and the other areas of our lives must fit around it.

That is where the harmful consequences become more evident. They may relate to relationships, jobs, finances, health, or something else. What harmful consequences have you experienced that could indicate a loss of control?

How has your life changed to serve a life-controlling problem? Are there any other signs that your practice/use may have progressed to the point of loss of control?

We have talked about three areas of symptoms: preoccupation, rituals, and loss of control. I think we can see how these are progressive. First, a substance or behavior fills our thoughts. Then that preoccupation leads to the development of rituals that may seem harmless—and yet those rituals lead directly to enslavement. As we let the rituals take over our lives, we are captured and mastered by our life-controlling problem.

Seeing this pattern in our lives and taking the steps necessary to break out of it is hard. As we begin to get past the symptoms, it is still dangerously easy to fall back into the preoccupation and isolation and too easy to let those "comfortable" rituals begin to reestablish themselves.

That is why our study this week on *perseverance* is so very important.

Another word for perseverance is ***endurance***. Can you think of some activities or sports that require physical endurance?

What do these activities have in common? Why do these require endurance? I can start well, but it is how I finish that determines my success

It is this same idea of enduring or "going the distance" that Peter writes about. Read 2 Peter 1:3-4.

Spiritual Awareness: Perseverance

In verse 5 we read, "For this very reason, make every effort to add to your faith goodness; to your goodness, knowledge; and to knowledge, self-control; and to self-control, *perseverance*" [emphasis added].

Can you see the progression here? We come to Christ in *faith;* and as we live out that faith, our lives are characterized by *goodness* (or moral excellence). As goodness is exercised, we develop a greater *knowledge* of who we are in Christ. Exercising that knowledge enables us to master our appetites and experience *self-control.*

Now we see that as we practice self-control, God will give us the ability to *persevere*—to patiently endure. The word perseverance here refers to the calm, determined, resolute, unflinching resolve to go with God.

Following are some additional verses that will help us better understand this spiritual objective of perseverance and how we can persevere as we work through the symptoms of a life-controlling problem.

Workbook: *Insight Group*, Turning Point, P. O. Box 22127, Chattanooga, TN 37422-2127

Hebrews 12:1-2
These verses come in the middle of a long passage about faith and perseverance. (It starts in Hebrews 10:19 and goes through most of chapter 13.) Was anyone curious enough when they read these verses to try to find out who the "great cloud of witnesses" was?

Because we are surrounded by so great a cloud of witnesses, lay aside every weight & sin that clings to us. Run with endurance, looking to Jesus, the founder & perfecter of our faith. He, for the joy set before Him, ~~for that~~ endured the cross, despising the shame. He is now at the RH of God

Verse 1 tells us what to do. What are the three things it mentions?

① lay aside weight & sin ② run with endurance. ③ look to Jesus the founder & perfecter of our faith

What does verse 2 tell us about ***how*** we can accomplish that?

Ephesians 6:10-18
God does not just tell us to persevere and then leave us alone to figure out how to accomplish that. These verses tell us how we can stand strong in our struggles. Let's look at the help He promises here.

Be strong in the Lord & in the strength of His might

Look at verse 10. Why is it so important for us to find our strength in the Lord?

That is the only way we can stand against the schemes of the devil

Do not forget who the enemy is. You cannot defeat him in your own strength, but God has provided some pretty thorough protection for us.

Do not wrestle against flesh & blood But against the rulers, authorities, cosmic powers over this present darkness. Against spiritual forces of evil in heavenly places

How much of our body is covered by this armor?

Head to Toe

What weapons does God give us in verses 17 and 18?

Sword of the Spirit = Word of God
praying in the Holy Spirit, perseverance

2 Corinthians 10:3-6
These verses continue the idea of spiritual warfare and the weapons God provides. They talk about weapons that are powerful enough to demolish strongholds. Do you remember what a stronghold is?

Weapons of divine power to destroy strongholds. Stronghold = arguments & lofty opinions raised AGAINST the knowledge of God

take every thought captive to obey Christ

What do these verses promise us about the power of these weapons as we use them in our struggle with a life-controlling problem?

They will destroy every stronghold.

Workbook: *Insight Group*, Turning Point, P. O. Box 22127, Chattanooga, TN 37422-2127

What does verse 5 have to say about our preoccupation with a life-controlling problem?

What does that statement have to say to the person whose mind is held captive by thoughts of a controlling addiction or dependency?

It is important to realize that our struggle with life-controlling problems is most often won or lost on the battlefield of the mind. A stronghold problem usually starts in the imagination. When we are preoccupied with a stronghold, our actions will surely follow; but when we take captive every thought to make it obedient to Christ, we are able to stand firm in our commitment to God.

Hebrews 10:35-36
How do these verses encourage us to persevere? How do they help us put our current struggles into an eternal perspective?

2 Timothy 2:12-13
These verses continue the idea of Hebrews 10 and encourage us to think in terms of eternity. What is the important word of encouragement in verse 13?

Philippians 1:6
The idea of perseverance implies an effort that endures "over the long haul." What does this verse say about God's commitment to us "over the long haul"?

Application

As we live out our faith in Christ, our lives are characterized by goodness (or moral excellence). As goodness is exercised, we develop a greater knowledge of who we are in Christ. Exercising that knowledge enables us to master our appetites and experience self-control.

As we practice self-control, God will give us the ability to persevere/patiently endure. The decision to persevere—to endure—is an *active* choice to *go with God*. Making that decision may involve reordering the priorities of our lives.

How can establishing proper priorities help us to persevere? Reread Hebrews 12:1-2.

Is something hindering you as you run the race or entangling you? What might that be?

Yes, God has provided us with an arsenal full of powerful weapons to fight with, but we have to make our own choices. He made us as beings with a free will. We can choose to go with God, or we can choose to go with the urges and desires of the flesh.

Those basic decisions we must make involve the choosing of priorities for our lives. How will we spend our time, where will we expend our energies, and—maybe most important—what will occupy our minds?

I would like for you to think about this whole area of priorities. How can you establish the kinds of priorities that will keep you "on track" over the long haul?

What priorities do you need to establish for your life?
How will you think and live differently if you follow those priorities?

In setting up those kinds of priorities and in making a solid commitment to persevere, we are taking a step of action to take back control of our lives; but we need to always keep in mind that this is *spiritual* warfare. We can make very sincere decisions about what we will and will not do; but aside from God's power in our lives, our best intentions will fail.

Workbook: *Insight Group*, Turning Point, P. O. Box 22127, Chattanooga, TN 37422-2127

Session 7 Ministry to One Another

Personal Preparation: Getting Ready for Session Seven

Meet With God

Personal Notes

I bow before the Father [illegible] whom every family in heaven & earth is named) that according to the riches of His glory, He may grant you strength and power thru His Spirit in your inner man so that Christ may dwell in your heart by faith – that you may be rooted and grounded in love may have strength to comprehend the breadth, length, height & depth [illegible] love of Christ so that you may be filled with the fulness of God. To Him be glory in the Church & in Christ Jesus

Are you setting aside time each day to meet with God alone? Give Him the opportunity to speak with you through His Word. Talk to Him in prayer about your daily struggles and the choices you face.

That process can be the source of great spiritual power and an important key to godly living. This week read Ephesians 3:14-21 for an important reminder of God's powerful love and 1 Timothy 6:6-19 for some help in the area of setting priorities.

Sharing Question

1 Tim 6:6-19 Godliness with contentment = great gain. Be content with what God has given. Flee desirousness of being rich. Pursue righteousness, godliness faith, love, steadfastness & gentleness

What is a good thing that is happening in your life right now, and what makes it good?

① Getting to know some Christian men better. We need each other.

② Sharing the Gospel with others – Great Commission Mk 16:15

Self-Awareness

No person is an island unto themselves. We need other people in our lives. Back when we talked about defenses, we looked at some of the dangers of isolating ourselves from one another. It is important to break down the walls that keep us from being known.

The format for this Self-Awareness time will provide group members the opportunity to share their story with the group.

Workbook: *Insight Group*, Turning Point, P. O. Box 22127, Chattanooga, TN 37422-2127

Over the past six weeks, we have talked together about many areas of our lives and struggles with life-controlling problems. We have discussed some important issues, and we have learned from each other's insights and observations.

Our Self-Awareness discussions have usually been centered around principles that we can use as we deal with the problem areas in our lives. Today, however, we are going to devote this time to a more personal focus.

As we enter this discussion, let us be aware of three primary resources God provides for us: The *Word of God* (Hebrews 4:12-13), the *Spirit of God* (John 16:13), and the *people of God* (Hebrews 3:13).

Over the past week, we have talked about some of the weapons God has provided for us in our growing walk of faith. We have talked about the value of God's Word and the guidance that His Holy Spirit makes available to us.

We have not said much about the third resource, and that is the people of God. God uses caring Christians in our lives just as He can use us in the lives of others. In Hebrews 3:13 we read, "But encourage one another daily, as long as it is called Today, so that none of you may be hardened by sin's deceitfulness."

Throughout the Bible, we find "one another" scriptures that instruct us in the kinds of caring actions and attitudes that ought to characterize our relationships as brothers and sisters in Christ. Let's look at a few of those "one another" verses.

1 Peter 1:22 says, "Love one another deeply, from the heart."

Galatians 5:13 tells us to "serve one another in love."

Galatians 6:2 points to a need: "Carry each other's burdens."

Ephesians 4:32 suggests an attitude: "Be kind and compassionate to one another." We will be looking at more of these "one another" verses over the weeks ahead because they are so very important. For now, let's allow the one another verses to set the tone as we begin a time of listening and sharing.

In this group session, two or three will share with us a brief history of a life-controlling problem or an awareness you have gained over the past weeks of an area where a life-controlling problem may have the potential of developing. This history could include specific examples of how a life-controlling problem has affected major areas of your life: your family, friends, health, job, school, hobbies, recreation, finances, or any other significant area. You may want to share a growing anticipation of a substance or behavior that could become a pattern leading to preoccupation.

Finally, I want you to tell us how you see God working in your life and what kind of progress you are experiencing in overcoming a life-controlling problem.

After each volunteer has spoken, we are going to ask a few questions, if we need to, that can help us better understand what we have heard.

The last step in the process will be for us to go around the group and ask each one to respond to what they have heard. Our purpose during this sharing time is not to judge or give advice but to be a Christian friend who cares enough to be honest.

Listen actively and, as you listen, ask yourself:

- Does this person have a clear understanding of how life-controlling problems develop?
- Are there feelings, defenses, denial, or blind areas that are hindering a clear view?
- What personal strengths do I see in this person that they may not be aware of?
- What evidence do I see of God at work in this life?

Workbook: *Insight Group*, Turning Point, P. O. Box 22127, Chattanooga, TN 37422-2127

We will begin this process in this group session and continue over the next two weeks until everyone has had an opportunity to speak. Before we get started, I would like to lay some ground rules.

First, *honesty* is essential—both in your sharing and in the response of group members. We must be honest. Even as we affirm each other, this is no place for the kind of empty flattery that can keep a person from clearly seeing a problem or the development of one.

Second, it is important to recognize the difference between *feedback* and *advice*. Our purpose in this sharing is simply to offer *feedback*, not to tell each other what to do. The best thing you can do for me is to help me see myself more clearly.

Third, our comments need to focus on *healing*, not *hurting*. Our aim is to support each other in love; so think in terms of encouragement, not tearing down. Along that line, it is important that we identify personal strengths we observe in each other.

Let me go over once more the "Ministry to One Another" format we will use:

1. Give us a brief history of a life-controlling problem and/or an awareness you have gained about the potential of such a problem. Do not give every detail but enough to help us understand.

2. Tell us how you feel a life-controlling problem is affecting the major areas of your life (relationships, health, job, recreation, money, and others that are significant) and/or what you will do with the awareness you have gained in the course.

3. Tell us whether you feel like you are making any progress in overcoming this stronghold.

4. Finally, tell us how you feel God is working in your life.

So, do we have any volunteers to start us off?

The rest of us are here as active listeners, and our goal is to *support* you in this process, not to judge or advise (NAME), I hope you sense that as you speak.

Okay, (NAME)...

Now each of you will have an opportunity to show your loving concern for (NAME) by offering some feedback about what you have heard.

Each group member is given the opportunity to offer a caring, clear, and constructive view.

I look forward to continuing this important process over the next two weeks. This kind of experience is valuable in two ways. First, it is helpful to our volunteers—and to all of us—as we use the principles we have learned and apply them to real life circumstances.

Our time is also valuable in the way it is a model of how we can help each other as members of the body of Christ to see ourselves more clearly. That insight into our blind areas is a valuable gift we can give to each other.

Can you think of other ways that caring Christian friends can help us walk with God?

In all those ways we have mentioned and many other ways we have not thought of, our fellow believers can help us live godly lives.

This whole area of living godly lives—being characterized by godliness—is the subject of our discussion for the next few minutes.

Workbook: *Insight Group*, Turning Point, P. O. Box 22127, Chattanooga, TN 37422-2127

Spiritual Awareness: Godliness

We find the word godliness in two different places in 2 Peter 1:3-11. Let's look at it together, starting with verse 3. What important statement about godliness do we find here?

Let's read verses 3 to 7.

Godliness means being like God in daily life. What are some of the characteristics you might see in the daily life of a person who is being "like God"?

Those are certainly characteristics we would want to see in our lives.

Another way to define godliness is "a devotion to God ***above all else***." What are some of the things in our lives—not necessarily bad things—that might compete for our devotion?

Even these good things can fill our days, take our time, and draw us away from our devotion to God.

Acts 3:1
Consistency of devotion to God is necessary for a life of godliness. What is the indication of Peter and John's consistent prayer life in this verse?

Daniel 6:10
Although Daniel's life could be taken, he continued to pray after a decree was given for no one to pray to another god for thirty days. This did not stop his devotion to God. What in the verse shows Daniel's consistency in his devotion to God?

1 Timothy 4:7b-8
Being physically fit is certainly a good thing, but here the importance of physical training is played down when compared to training in ***godliness***. Can you find anything in these verses that shows us how physical training is limited when it is compared to training in godliness?

How does the promise in verse 8 motivate you toward godliness? Do we work as hard at training in godliness as we work at taking care of our physical health and well-being?

2 Peter 3:10-13
What does verse 11 say to us when we get caught up in the things this world values—things like possessions, importance, bank accounts, and leisure—and let them extinguish our desire for holiness and the things of God?

Workbook: *Insight Group*, Turning Point, P. O. Box 22127, Chattanooga, TN 37422-2127

1 Timothy 6:11
The verse before this one talks about all the trouble that the love of money and the lifelong pursuit of money can lead to, but the writer tells us to flee all of that. Instead, he presents a challenge to other pursuits. What does he encourage us to pursue?

Righteousness, godliness, faith, love, steadfastness, and gentleness

We have come across these before! Which ones are in the 2 Peter 1 passage? = righteousness, knowledge, self control, affection, love

Faith, virtue (moral excellence) steadfastness, godliness, brotherly

And how do we get these into our lives?

Pursue implies some concentrated effort. We must pursue them—that is our part. And God's part? Well, He has provided us with three resources that can enable us to experience godliness (and these other qualities) in our lives. I will mention them again: the Word of God, the Spirit of God, and the people of God.

The Holy Spirit is an important resource God has provided for us in our pursuit of godliness.

John 14:26; 16:13
What do these verses tell us about what the Holy Spirit will do for us?

Jn 14:26 Teach us all things, bring to our remembrance all Jesus said to us.

John 16:13 Guide us into all truth, + declare to us the things to come

Have you experienced a time when you felt that God's Spirit in you was guiding you toward godliness (away from the urges of the flesh) or when He brought God's truth to your mind when you needed it?

patience vs frustration

God is willing and able to respond to our cries for help—but if prayer is such a powerful resource, why should we keep it on a shelf except for the occasional crisis?

Philippians 4:6
When is prayer the appropriate response to a difficulty, question, temptation, or other situation?

Always – in everything, by prayer and supplication with thanksgiving, let your requests be made known unto God

2 Timothy 3:1-5
In this passage Paul talks about the increase of ungodliness in the last days. We see the lack of character. The path to character or godliness is one of being real, not putting on a religious mask. What in verse 5 indicates an appearance of godliness but no inner strength?

Having the appearance of godliness, but denying its power

Can you remember the three resources God gives us to enable us to live godly lives? What are they? Word, Spirit, Other Believers

Workbook: *Insight Group*, Turning Point, P. O. Box 22127, Chattanooga, TN 37422-2127

Application

It is important for us to remember that—just like with self-control or perseverance—godliness will not *just happen* in our lives. We will not accidently fall into a godly lifestyle—the flesh and the devil will see to that!

Godliness must be pursued. We must train for it. While some of that training can take place in church, in bible studies, and in groups like this one, much of the work must be done one-on-one—alone with God.

The process is simple. We read God's Word, asking His Spirit to guide us into its truth. We meditate on God's Word (let it sink in). Then in prayer, we ask God to use the truth of His Word to cut to our hearts.

The prayer part is simple too. We talk to God. We ask for what we need. We thank Him.

You have been encouraged through these past six weeks to begin making time alone with God a regular part of your daily life. If you have not yet made a commitment to do that, make this the day you begin.

Why do you think it is important to set specific and regular times for personal time with God? If not several (many) days will pass w.o. spending time alone with God.

What can you do or change to make this happen in your life?
Plan for it. Go to bed on time, set the alarm, & get up.

What do you believe God can do *for* you and *in* you during a time alone each day? Give wisdom, direction, power, and a deep awareness of His presence

As you talk to God this week, ask Him to give you the self-control and perseverance to be faithful to your daily appointment. Your reward will be a growing and consistent personal relationship with Him and a life that is characterized by godliness.

Session 8

Ministry to One Another Continuation

Personal Preparation: Getting Ready for Session Eight

Meet With God

Personal Notes

Have you found the time and place that works best for your daily time alone with God? When you pray this week, remember specific needs that have been mentioned by other group members. You can have a significant ministry in their lives as you pray for them.

During your time in God's Word, read some stories Jesus told as they are recorded in Luke 15. They give us a picture of how important each one of us is to God.

Sharing Question

What is the one thing about this group that you value the most?

Self-Awareness

During our Self-Awareness time, we are going to continue with the ministry to one another we began last week. Once again, I am going to invite several volunteers to tell us how you have been affected by a life-controlling problem or what you have learned through the weeks we have been meeting about an area where a life-controlling problem could be developing. We would like to know whether you feel like you have made any progress in being an overcomer and how you feel God is working in your life.

Workbook: *Insight Group*, Turning Point, P. O. Box 22127, Chattanooga, TN 37422-2127

Before we start, I want to remind us of the ground rules for this session:

1. Honesty is important.

2. This feedback is not advice. Our goal is to provide a "reality check" for each other to help us see ourselves more clearly and to see into our own blind areas.

3. Our focus is on helping, not hurting. Our aim is encouragement.

You remember how we talked last time about the ministry we can have to one another. The Word of God, the Spirit of God, and the people of God are three important resources God provides for us as we make it our goal to live godly lives.

This is the kind of ministry God wants us to have toward each other. Read these verses and write down your thoughts.

Romans 15:7 tells us to accept one another. Welcome one another (as Christ welcomed you) for the glory of God

1 John 4:7 and 11 show that we are to love one another as God loved us. Love one another for love is from God. Whoever loves has been born of God and knows God.

1 Corinthians 12:25 indicates that our relationship should be one of concern for each other. that there would be no divisions in the body, but that we should have the same care for one another.

Let's keep these truths in mind as we continue our ministry to one another in the next few minutes.

As we did last week, we will be asking each group member to provide feedback in the form of constructive comments. Does this person have a life-controlling problem or an understanding of such problems? Do they see the effects of life-controlling problems clearly? Finally, what personal strengths do they have that they may not be aware of?

We will ask for volunteers to start us off today.

We'll have more time next week for others to have their turn at this very useful process of ministry to one another. Now it is time to move into our study based on 2 Peter 1.

faith, virtue, knowledge, self-control, steadfastness, godliness, brotherly affection, love.

Spiritual Awareness: Brotherly Kindness

In verse 7 we read, “And to [your] godliness, [add] brotherly kindness.”

It is not hard to imagine how a person who has developed the quality of godliness would begin to reflect God’s attitude outwardly—to the people around them.

Brotherly kindness here specifically relates to kindness exercised *within the family of God*. It involves caring for our brothers and sisters in Christ. It is affection that grows out of common interests and concern—and those commonalities draw us together.

In what ways do you think brotherly kindness would show itself? What kinds of attitudes and actions would result from brotherly kindness? Should be much deeper than the world experiences – By this shall all men know you are my disciples, if you have love one for another.

What have you witnessed in our ministry to one another time that are examples of brotherly kindness?

Genuine concern for the needs of one another

Let’s see what else God’s Word has to say about the subject of kindness and compassion toward our brothers and sisters in the faith.

Romans 12:10

What does this say about the degree of our love for other Christians? Outdo one another in showing honor

---

How would you put that verse into action? Mt 5:41 If any one forces you to go one mile, go with him two miles. Enemy forces, but for a brother we go many miles.

Luke 10:33-35

The Samaritan in Jesus’ story is an example of brotherly kindness. Jesus used this story to explain what He meant when He said, “Love your neighbor as yourself” (v.27). Is this neighborly kindness?

We can learn from the example of the Samaritan about how to show brotherly kindness and compassion for others.

What are some of the things the Samaritan did for this man in trouble? poured in wine & oil,

What is the *first* thing he did? In compassion, he bound up his wounds,

Then what action did he take? Set him upon his animal, brought him to an inn, and took care of him. Next day, he gave the innkeeper money saying take care of him and whatever more you spend, I will repay you when I return

What does this example say to you about the people around you who are in trouble? As led by God, help them.

1 Peter 1:22
How does this verse describe the love that we demonstrate within the body of Christ? Fervent love from a pure heart

Seeing you have purified your souls in obeying the truth thru the Spirit unto sincere love for the brethren, love one another with a pure heart fervently.

Hebrews 10:24-25
How can we spur one another on toward love and good deeds?
Attending our ~~assemblies~~ meetings, as some do, and encourage one another all the more as the Day of Jesus' Return nearing

What two instructions do we find in verse 25? Why are they important? (a) meet together
(b) encourage each other, even more so as
We need each other.

What indicates that some people may have been withdrawing or isolating themselves? as is the habit of some

John 13:34-35
These words are found among Christ's final instructions to His disciples, and that gives them some added emphasis. How do we know that Jesus is not just making a casual suggestion here? A new commandment I give you

How are we to love one another? As Christ loved us – this is the new part

He is the example for the kind of love for one another that should characterize our lives.

What is so unique about the love of Christians that Jesus could say in verse 35, "All men will know that you are my disciples, if you love one another"? What kinds of things do we do in showing Christian love and brotherly kindness that grab the attention of those outside of the faith? Unselfish love – not for something we get.

Galatians 6:10
Let's end our study time with this verse that summarizes so well the meaning and practice of brotherly kindness.

Where does it tell us to focus our special efforts? Especially, the house hold of faith. (Because this will allow us also to show God's love to the unbelievers.)

Application

The Galatians 6:10 passage talks about *opportunity*: "As we have opportunity, let us do good..." What kind of opportunities might you have this week to do good to those who belong to the family of God?

Encourage with a simple visit. Share a truth I've learned — receive an insight, which will strengthen the bod

Someone once said that while you might not have a chance to do a *great* thing for someone today (rescue someone from a fire or a small child from drowning), there are many opportunities for small acts of kindness that can make a difference in someone's life.

Can you think of some of those small opportunities you might have?

Why isn't this ***more*** a part of our lives?

What would happen in the body of Christ (in our church) if we each began to live lives that were characterized by compassion and brotherly kindness? We would be the Church

How would it build up the body of Christ?

The eye needs the hand, the feet need the ears, etc

Workbook: *Insight Group*, Turning Point, P. O. Box 22127, Chattanooga, TN 37422-2127

Session 9

Ministry to One Another Conclusion

Personal Preparation: Getting Ready for Session Nine

Meet With God

Personal Notes

During these final weeks of *Insight Group* meetings, there has been much to think about and digest. Talk to God about your personal struggles. Also, mentally go around the circle of your *Insight Group* and pray for each one. Our study this week is on godly love. These two passages will prepare you for this study. Read and think about Romans 8:32-39 and 1 Corinthians 13.

He gave His Son will He not also give us all things we need. Who shall bring a charge against a brother (God's elect). God justifies. He will condemn. Christ died for us & is at the right hand of God and is interceding for us. Nothing can separate us from the love of God, which is in Christ Jesus. We are more than conquerors thru Him, who loved us. Tho we have all gifts — w/o love nothing. Love never ends. Prophecy, tongues, knowledge will pass away. We know in part, prophesy in part. When the perfect comes, the partial will pass away. What will last? faith, hope & love. Love is the greatest

Sharing Question

What is one quality that you value or admire in one or more members of this group? Love of God & love for each other

Self-Awareness

Our weeks together as a group—especially the "ministry to one another" process—have provided a valuable model for us as they help us understand what *Christian community* is all about. We have seen how caring brothers and sisters in Christ can *minister* to us—and how we, in turn, can reach out to others.

Have the other group members had a positive impact on your life? In what ways? Sharing scriptural insights and the impact of the Word in their lives

Workbook: *Insight Group*, Turning Point, P. O. Box 22127, Chattanooga, TN 37422-2127

In this session, we are going to continue our ministry to one another for those who have not yet had their opportunity to share a brief history of a life-controlling problem or an awareness of a potentially life-controlling problem in some area of your life. You may talk about how important areas of your life such as relationships, job, finances, health, recreation time, social life, or any other areas may be affected.

As we have been doing the past two weeks, we are going to ask the others in the group to offer clear, constructive, and encouraging feedback.

We find our model for this peer ministry in verses throughout the Bible that teach us the ways we can express our love for one another. Let's look at a few more of these important verses.

---

1 Thessalonians 4:18 instructs us to encourage (KJV says "comfort") one another.

James 5:16 tells us to confess our sins to one another and pray for each other.

Colossians 3:13 says to bear with each other and forgive one another.

Hebrews 3:13 instructs us to encourage one another daily (regularly), as long as it is called Today (implies an urgency), so that none of you may be hardened by sin's deceitfulness.

Let's keep these thoughts in our minds as we begin our sharing time.

Before we start, I need to remind us all of the ground rules:

1. Honesty is important.

2. Feedback is *not* advice. Our purpose in sharing is to provide honest feedback about what we hear and to help each other see more of the areas (blind areas) that may have been hidden by walls of defense or denial.

3. Our focus is on helping and healing, not on tearing down. Our ultimate aim is to encourage.

We will continue our ministry to one another.

As everyone has been given the opportunity to experience feedback, I hope you have felt God's love in a very practical and tangible way through the caring and concern of the other group members.

Can you think of something you heard or witnessed during this ministry to one another that made God's love more real to you?

Spiritual Awareness: Love

As we look together into 2 Peter 1 for our final study together, let's move to verse 7 where we read, "[Add] to [your] brotherly kindness, *love*." This is the top rung on this ladder of Christian character.

I think this would be a good time to review briefly the eight objectives (or qualities) that God wants to see us develop.

The foundation is saving *faith*—repentance for sin and a personal commitment to Jesus Christ. As we exercise faith in Christ, we develop goodness. Goodness leads us to a practical *knowledge* of who we are in Christ; and based on the right thinking that grows out of that knowledge, we are able to practice self-control over the urges that try to master us.

As we exercise self-control, God gives us the strength to persevere. That perseverance or endurance leads to a godly lifestyle. And that *godliness* begins to show itself through a life that is characterized by *kindness* to others—especially to other Christians.

Finally, we come to the deep love for others that Peter talks about in verse 7.

This love extends to all who are in the body of Christ and beyond. It is Godlike love. God's love working through us helps us love the unlovable.

Let's look at some of the characteristics of this love.

John 3:16
How does this loving act—God giving His own Son—show a love that is different from human love?

This is our model of the kind of love that should be our goal. It is a sacrificial and self-giving love.

1 John 4:7-12
Where does this love come from? From God! Every one who loves is born of God. He who doesn't love does not know God. Because God is love. This is love — not that we loved God — but He loved us and gave His Son. God loved us — we should love one another.

Why are we to love others? No one has seen God. If we love, they can see Him in us

Galatians 2:20
What happens in our lives that enables us to show this supernatural love—love that goes far beyond what we are capable of in our own strength? We are crucified with Christ. The lives we now live are not our own but Christ's

I can't. He can. I can do all things thru Christ who gives me strength

Romans 5:7-8
Do we deserve God's love toward us? Hardly would one die for a good or righteous person, but Christ died for me while I was in sin

Do we love people because they deserve it? No

What motivates our love? God loves them + I want to be like Him

1 Corinthians 13
This chapter tells us a great deal about love. What are some of the characteristics of a person who demonstrates *godly* love? patient, kind, does not envy does not boast, not arrogant, not rude, doesn't insist on their own way, not irritable nor resentful, does not rejoice in wrong doing but in the truth, bears all things, believes all things, hopes all things, endures all things, NEVER ENDS

In this chapter we read about some spiritual gifts and such qualities as faith, generosity, even martyrdom. Then it says unless these qualities are based in *love*, they are nothing. Everything else, including our faith and hope, will one day pass away. (When we see the real thing in heaven, we will not need to have *faith* or to *hope* because then we can know and we can see.) But even then, love will continue to be at the center of our relationship with God and with our fellow believers.

Love is the finished product of our eight objectives. Let's return to 2 Peter 1 and read it together beginning with Peter's greeting in verse 2. I hope that through the repetitions over these weeks, God has imprinted these words on your hearts.

Workbook: *Insight Group*, Turning Point, P. O. Box 22127, Chattanooga, TN 37422-2127

This is how our faith grows beyond saving faith to become a way of life. I hope you will return to these verses again and again in your personal study and let God remind you of what you have learned.

Application

Our question now is: Where do we go from here? Though this is the end of these nine sessions together, it is certainly *not* the end of the process that God has begun in each of our lives.

Our Spiritual Awareness time today has focused on *love*, and that is where I would like to begin to talk about our strategies for the future.

How can we extend God's love to others who struggle with life-controlling problems?

What plans have you begun to formulate for reaching out to others?

While maintaining confidentiality, can you tell us about the ways you believe God would have you reach out to another person who has the symptoms of a life-controlling problem?

Your personal awareness of life-controlling problems and their symptoms has uniquely prepared you to reach out in love to others who have needs in their lives.

Workbook: *Insight Group*, Turning Point, P. O. Box 22127, Chattanooga, TN 37422-2127

The Plan of Salvation

Is there any good reason why you cannot receive Jesus Christ right now?

How to receive Christ:

1. Admit your need (that you are a sinner).

2. Be willing to turn from your sins (repent).

3. Believe that Jesus Christ died for you on the cross and rose from the grave.

4. Through prayer, invite Jesus Christ to come in and control your life through the Holy Spirit (receive Him as Savior and Lord).

What to Pray

Dear God,
I know that I am a sinner and need Your forgiveness.
I believe that Jesus Christ died for my sins.
I am willing to turn from my sins.
I now invite Jesus Christ to come into my heart and life as my personal Savior.
I am willing, by God's strength, to follow and obey Jesus Christ as the Lord of my life.

Date Signature

The Bible says: "Everyone who calls on the name of the Lord will be saved." *Romans 10:13*

"Yet to all who received him, to those who believed in his name, he gave the right to become children of God." *John 1:12*

"Therefore, since we have been justified through faith, we have peace with God through our Lord Jesus Christ." *Romans 5:1*

When we receive Christ, we are born into the family of God through the supernatural work of the Holy Spirit who lives within every believer. This process is called regeneration or the new birth.

Share your decision to receive Christ with another person.

Connect to a local church.

Selected Bibliography

Augsburger, David. *Caring Enough to Confront.* Glendale: Regal Books, 1980.

Carnes, Patrick. *Out of the Shadows: Understanding Sexual Addiction.* Minneapolis: CompCare Publishers, 1983.

Cook, Jerry, and Stanley C. Baldwin. *Love, Acceptance and Forgiveness.* Glendale: Regal Books, 1979.

Crabb, Lawrence J. *Effective Biblical Counseling.* Grand Rapids: Zondervan Publishing House, 1977.

______________. *Connecting.* Nashville: Thomas Nelson Publishing, 2005.

Gorman, Julie A. *Community That Is Christian: A Handbook on Small Groups.* Wheaton: Victor Books, 1993.

Hart, Archibald. *Counseling the Depressed.* Dallas: Word Publishing, 1987.

Hemfelt, Robert, Frank Minirth, and Paul Meier. *Love Is A Choice—Recovery for Codependent Relationships.* Nashville: Thomas Nelson Publishers, 1989.

Hestenes, Roberta. *Using the Bible in Groups.* Philadelphia: The Westminster Press, 1983.

Icenogle, Gareth Weldon. *Biblical Foundations for Small Groups.* Downers Grove, IL: InterVarsity Press, 1994.

Johnson, Vernon E. *I'll Quit Tomorrow.* San Francisco: Harper and Row Publishers, 1980.

Lee, Jimmy Ray. *Understanding the Times and Knowing What to Do.* Chattanooga, TN: Turning Point Ministries, 1997.

Luft, Joseph. *Group Processes: An Introduction to Group Dynamics.* Mountainview, CA: Mayfield Publishing Company, 1984.

May, Gerald G. *Addiction and Grace.* San Francisco: Harper and Row Publishers, 1988.

Miller, J. Keith. *Sin: Overcoming the Ultimate Deadly Addiction.* San Francisco: Harper and Row Publishers, 1987.

Minirth, Frank, Paul Meier, Robert Hemfelt, and Sharon Sneed. *Love Hunger.* Nashville: Thomas Nelson Publishers, 1990.

Minirth, Frank, Paul Meier, Siegfried Fink, Walter Byrd, and Don Hawkins. *Taking Control.* Grand Rapids: Baker Book House, 1988.

O'Gorman, Patricia, and Philip Oliver-Diaz. *Breaking the Cycle of Addiction.* Deerfield Beach: Health Communications, 1987.

Perkins, Bill. *Fatal Attractions: Overcoming Our Secret Addictions.* Eugene: Harvest House, 1991.

Schaumburg, Harry W. *False Intimacy.* Colorado Springs: Navpress, 1992.

Stanley, Charles F. *Handle with Prayer.* Wheaton: Victor Books, 1988.

Thurman, Chris. *The Lies We Believe.* Nashville: Thomas Nelson Publishers, 1989.

VanVonderen, Jeff. *Good News for the Chemically Dependent.* Nashville: Thomas Nelson Publishers, 1985.

Vath, Raymond E. *Counseling Those with Eating Disorders.* Waco: World Books, 1986.

Wilson, Sandra D. *Counseling Adult Children of Alcoholics.* Dallas: Word Publishing, 1989.

We'd love to hear from you!

I hope your life has been changed in some way during these past weeks. If you would like to share how God has touched your life through this group, please send us your thoughts. A personal testimony of God's love will honor Him and could encourage others to reach out for help. Also, we would love to celebrate your victories with you!

May we shout for joy when we hear of your victory
and raise a banner in the name of our God (Psalm 20:5 NLT).

We would also appreciate your suggestions for how we might improve the curriculum.

Three ways to send us your comments:

Email:
info@livingfree.org

Postal mail:
Living Free
P. O. Box 22127
Chattanooga, TN 37422-2127

Fax:
423-899-4547

May God richly bless you as you continue your journey with Him.

Jimmy R. Lee, D.Min.
President

Living Free®
Discovering God's Path to Freedom

To learn more about Living Free, please visit us at www.LivingFree.org.

- Shop in our bookstore
- Guidelines for small groups
- Read about new curriculum
- Help for facilitators
- Discussion forums
- Help for life's problems

Has Living Free made a difference in your life? Would you like to help others receive similar blessings?

Prayer

More than anything, we desire your prayers for the ministry of Living Free. We can work hard, write excellent curriculum, and offer great training experiences; but none of this can be effective without the power of the Holy Spirit. God is the one who changes people's lives. Our prayer partners receive periodic prayer requests for the ministry by email.

Mission

Jimmy Lee and Dan Strickland make several international trips each year—training, making ministry contacts, and assisting ministries desiring to develop Living Free groups in their country. Some of these trips will be open to individuals or groups. We will be looking for trained and experienced Living Free facilitators as well as people wanting to join a work team for a mission service project or medical mission.

Support

God is opening doors for Living Free ministry around world, and we are moving through those doors by faith. We are excited and thankful for the growth, but growth brings new financial challenges. Our Giving Partners help us continue and expand the ministry.

If you are interested in getting involved, please contact us

Email:
info@livingfree.org

Postal mail:
Living Free
P. O. Box 22127
Chattanooga, TN 37422-2127